Jemima Love Bible Stories

Job's Jemima

Written by Nicole Deanes Mangum

Illustrated by Brittany Nicole Deanes

Copyright © 2006; 2009 2023 Nicole Deanes Mangum

Jemima Love Bible Stories is a series of bible stories penned by Nicole Deanes Mangum aka Jemima Love

Illustrated by Brittany Nicole Deanes

3rd Edition

All rights reserved. No part of this publication may be reproduced, distributed, or transmitted in any form or by any means, including photocopying, recording, or other electronic or mechanical methods, without the prior written permission of the publisher, except in the case of brief quotations embodied in critical reviews and certain other noncommercial uses permitted by copyright law.

ISBN- 978-1-951300-67-8

Liberation's Publishing – 183 Cottrell St. - West Point, MS 1-800-325-8028

Dedication

This book is dedicated to teachers everywhere.
Where would we be without you?

Today is Jemima Love's first day,

to teach the class at Latter Rain.

The children here are kind of rude,

and life has treated them unkind and crude.

Jemima Love will change their story.

She'll set them on the path to glory.

In she goes, and you'd best believe

immediately they start to tease.

"Jemima!?" Called out Hakim.

"Like the pancake lady. Oh please!"

"No," said Kizzy. "She is our maid.

All she needs is a red scarf and braids."

"A maid," laughed Jemima. "That is very cute.

It's a shame that you don't know the truth.

Jemima was not a slave, and definitely not a maid.

Jemima's from the bible if you didn't know.

She was the eldest daughter of Job."

"The daughter of Job," all the children cried.

"The storm killed his children. We read it last night."

"My dear children had you continued to read

you would have learned Job was redeemed.

I will tell you the story, so settle down.

The story of Job, the big man about town."

There was a man from the land of Uz

not a one could fill his boots.

He was perfect, upright, and bold.

He feared God and did what he was told.

His substance was camel, oxen, and sheep

hundreds and thousands fold he'd keep.

His children always had great feast.

There Dad was the greatest in all the East.

Once all their feasting and fun was gone

Job would sacrifice for their wrong.

He'd give burnt offering to the Lord

in case they unknowingly cursed God in their heart.

The people of the land all called Job blessed

When they saw him this they'd confess.

Job fed the orphans and stood up for their rights.

He gave them a safe place to sleep at night.

He'd cause the widows heart to sing

from all the blessings he would bring.

Job hated a thief and once taken down
he'd take their gold right out of their mouths.

Job loved the Lord, and the Lord loved his boy.
For this Satan came to steal, kill, and destroy.
The sons of God gathered before God's throne.
In comes Satan plotting wrong.

The Lord asked, "What is it Satan? Why are you here?
Have you set your eyes on the one I hold dear?"

Satan the accuser started in on Job.

He said, "Job loves you because of all he owns.
Take away the hedge. Let me go in.
I know he will curse you and sin."

"Go ahead," said the Lord. "Test him you may.
My Job will be faithful. He will not turn away."

Satan took Job's children and his wealth,
And last but not least he took Job's health.

Job's wife said, "Just curse God and die."
"You foolish woman," Job replied.
"The Lord giveth and he taketh away,
And I will love him either way."

Job's friends said, "Job you must have done wrong

now God has taken all you own."

No one in Job's life understood

he suffered not because of wrong, but good.

For Job's faithfulness he was repaid

double for his trouble in his old age.

In that blessing he did receive

the most beautiful daughters in the entire east

Keren, Kezia, and Jemima, like me.

King James Version of the book of Job
Illustrations taken from the 1ˢᵗ Edition of Job's Jemima

Job 1:1-12 KJV

There was a man in the land of Uz, whose name was Job; and that man was perfect and upright, and one that feared God, and eschewed evil.
² And there were born unto him seven sons and three daughters.
³ His substance also was seven thousand sheep, and three thousand camels, and five hundred yoke of oxen, and five hundred she asses, and a very great household; so that this man was the greatest of all the men of the east.
⁴ And his sons went and feasted in their houses, every one his day; and sent and called for their three sisters to eat and to drink with them.
⁵ And it was so, when the days of their feasting were gone about, that Job sent and sanctified them, and rose up early in the morning, and offered burnt offerings according to the number of them all: for Job said, It may be that my sons have sinned, and cursed God in their hearts. Thus did Job continually.
⁶ Now there was a day when the sons of God came to present themselves before the Lord, and Satan came also among them.
⁷ And the Lord said unto Satan, Whence comest thou? Then Satan answered the Lord, and said, From going to and fro in the earth, and from walking up and down in it.
⁸ And the Lord said unto Satan, Hast thou considered my servant Job, that there is none like him in the earth, a perfect and an upright man, one that feareth God, and escheweth evil?
⁹ Then Satan answered the Lord, and said, Doth Job fear God for nought?

¹⁰ Hast not thou made an hedge about him, and about his house, and about all that he hath on every side? thou hast blessed the work of his hands, and his substance is increased in the land.

¹¹ But put forth thine hand now, and touch all that he hath, and he will curse thee to thy face.

¹² And the Lord said unto Satan, Behold, all that he hath is in thy power; only upon himself put not forth thine hand. So Satan went forth from the presence of the Lord.

Job 29:11-12 KJV

11 When the ear heard me, then it blessed me; and when the eye saw me, it gave witness to me:

12 Because I delivered the poor that cried, and the fatherless, and him that had none to help him.

Job 29:13 KJV

3 The blessing of him that was ready to perish came upon me: and I caused the widow's heart to sing for joy.

Job 29:14-17

14 I put on righteousness, and it clothed me: my judgment was as a robe and a diadem.
15 I was eyes to the blind, and feet was I to the lame.
16 I was a father to the poor: and the cause which I knew not I searched out.
17 And I brake the jaws of the wicked, and plucked the spoil out of his teeth.

Job 2:1-10 KJV

1 Again there was a day when the sons of God came to present themselves before the LORD, and Satan came also among them to present himself before the LORD.
2 And the LORD said unto Satan, From whence comest thou? And Satan answered the LORD, and said, From going to and fro in the earth, and from walking up and down in it.
3 And the LORD said unto Satan, Hast thou considered my servant Job, that there is none like him in the earth, a perfect and an upright man, one that feareth God, and escheweth evil? and still he holdeth fast his integrity, although thou movedst me against him, to destroy him without cause.
4 And Satan answered the LORD, and said, Skin for skin, yea, all that a man hath will he give for his life. 25
5 But put forth thine hand now, and touch his bone and his flesh, and he will curse thee to thy face.
6 And the LORD said unto Satan, Behold, he is in thine hand; but save his life.
7 So went Satan forth from the presence of the LORD, and smote Job with sore boils from the sole of his foot unto his crown.
8 And he took him a potsherd to scrape himself withal; and he sat down among the ashes.
9 Then said his wife unto him, Dost thou still retain thine integrity? curse God, and die.
10 But he said unto her, Thou speakest as one of the foolish women speaketh. What? shall we receive good at the hand of God, and shall we not receive evil? In all this did not Job sin with his lips.

Job 2:11

11 Now when Job's three friends heard of all this evil that was come upon him, they came every one from his own place; Eliphaz the Temanite, and Bildad the Shuhite, and Zophar the Naamathite: for they had made an appointment together to come to mourn with him and to comfort him.

Job 16:1-2

1 Then Job answered and said, 2 I have heard many such things: miserable comforters are ye all.

Job 19:1-5

1 Then Job answered and said,
2 How long will ye vex my soul, and break me in pieces with words?
3 These ten times have ye reproached me: ye are not ashamed that ye make yourselves strange to me.
4 And be it indeed that I have erred, mine error remaineth with myself.
5 If indeed ye will magnify yourselves against me, and plead against me my reproach:

Job 42:1-10

1 Then Job answered the LORD, and said,
2 I know that thou canst do every thing, and that no thought can be with holden from thee.
3 Who is he that hideth counsel without knowledge? therefore have I uttered that I understood not; things too wonderful for me, which I knew not.
4 Hear, I beseech thee, and I will speak: I will demand of thee, and declare thou unto me.
5 I have heard of thee by the hearing of the ear: but now mine eye seeth thee.
6 Wherefore I abhor myself, and repent in dust and ashes.
7 And it was so, that after the LORD had spoken these words unto Job, the

LORD said to Eliphaz the Temanite, My wrath is kindled against thee, and against thy two friends: for ye have not spoken of me the thing that is right, as my servant Job hath.

8 Therefore take unto you now seven bullocks and seven rams, and go to my servant Job, and offer up for yourselves a burnt offering; and my servant Job shall pray for you: for him will I accept: lest I deal with you after your folly, in that ye have not spoken of me the thing which is right, like my servant Job.

9 So Eliphaz the Temanite and Bildad the Shuhite and Zophar the Naamathite went, and did according as the LORD commanded them: the LORD also accepted Job.

10 And the LORD turned the captivity of Job, when he prayed for his friends: also the LORD gave Job twice as much as he had before

Job 42:12-17

12 So the LORD blessed the latter end of Job more than his beginning: for he had fourteen thousand sheep, and six thousand camels, and a thousand yoke of oxen, and a thousand she asses.

13 He had also seven sons and three daughters.

14 And he called the name of the first, Jemima; and the name of the second, Kezia; and the name of the third, Kerenhappuch.

15 And in all the land were no women found so fair as the daughters of Job: and their father gave them inheritance among their brethren.

16 After this lived Job an hundred and forty years, and saw his sons, and his sons' sons, even four generations.

17 So Job died, being old and full of days.

Notes

www.ingramcontent.com/pod-product-compliance
Lightning Source LLC
Chambersburg PA
CBHW040759240426
43673CB00014B/396